# TORONTO
# MAPLE LEAFS

**BY LUKE HANLON**

Book design by Maggie Villaume
Cover design by Maggie Villaume

Photographs ©: Frank Gunn/The Canadian Press/AP Images, cover; Steven Kingsman/Icon Sportswire, 4–5, 9; Sean Kilpatrick/The Canadian Press/AP Images, 7; Shutterstock Images, 10–11; AP Images, 13, 15, 16–17, 19, 21; IHA/Icon Sportswire, 23; Rusty Kennedy/Bernie Parent/AP Images, 24–25; Mark J. Terrill/AP Images, 27; Gerry Angus/Icon Sportswire, 29

Press Box Books, an imprint of Press Room Editions.

**ISBN**
978-1-63494-498-4 (library bound)
978-1-63494-524-0 (paperback)
978-1-63494-575-2 (epub)
978-1-63494-550-9 (hosted ebook)

**Library of Congress Control Number: 2022902483**

Distributed by North Star Editions, Inc.
2297 Waters Drive
Mendota Heights, MN 55120
www.northstareditions.com

Printed in the United States of America
082022

## ABOUT THE AUTHOR

Luke Hanlon is a sportswriter from Minneapolis.

# TABLE OF CONTENTS

# 1

Auston Matthews shoots the puck during his first NHL game.

# A DEBUT FOR THE AGES

Auston Matthews skated into the crease. The 19-year-old was playing in his first National Hockey League (NHL) game. Matthews and the Toronto Maple Leafs were on the road against the Ottawa Senators. Leafs teammate William Nylander sent a swift pass toward the young center. But a Senators defender lifted Matthews's stick before he could get a shot off.

Toronto forward Zach Hyman took control of the loose puck. He passed it to Matthews in front of the net. This time, Matthews fired the puck past goalie Craig Anderson. He scored!

The Maple Leafs had taken Matthews with the first pick in the 2016 draft. Fans in Toronto had become used to disappointment. The Leafs had missed the playoffs in 10 of the previous 11 seasons. This put extra pressure on Matthews to succeed. It took him less than nine minutes to prove he could handle the pressure.

Later in the first period, Senators defenseman Erik Karlsson gained control of the puck. But Matthews sneaked up

Matthews celebrates after scoring a goal in his first game with the Leafs.

behind him. He lifted Karlsson's stick, stole the puck away, and raced down the left wing. Matthews fired a wrist shot. It flew between Anderson's legs and into the net.

In the second period, Leafs defenseman Morgan Rielly streaked down the left side of the ice. He passed the puck to Matthews, who stood unguarded in front of the goal. Matthews buried an easy one-timer. It was his third goal of the night. That made him only the seventh player in NHL history to record a hat trick in his debut. And he wasn't done yet.

Later in the second, Matthews and Nylander sprang a two-on-one breakaway. At the last moment, Nylander passed the

## MEMORABLE MEMORABILIA

Craig Anderson's performance in goal was one he'd probably like to forget. Even so, Anderson knew he was a part of history. After the game, he asked Matthews to sign his stick. Matthews wrote, "Thanks 'four' making my first game memorable."

Matthews scores his fourth goal of the night against Ottawa goalie Craig Anderson.

puck. Matthews put it in the back of the net. That made him the first player since 1917 to score four goals in his debut.

The Maple Leafs ended up losing the game in overtime 5–4. But Toronto fans knew they had a superstar on their hands.

# 2

The Leafs began playing their home games at Maple Leaf Gardens in 1931.

# BECOMING THE MAPLE LEAFS

The NHL formed in 1917. That season, four Canadian teams made up the league. The Toronto franchise was originally known as the Arenas. They played their first game on December 19, 1917. It was a 10–9 loss to the Montreal Wanderers. However, the Arenas went on to reach the Stanley Cup Final that year. In Game 5, right winger Alf Skinner tallied two goals and an assist.

That helped the Arenas defeat the Vancouver Millionaires 2–1. The Arenas became the first Stanley Cup champions of the NHL era.

Two years after that triumph, new owners bought the franchise. They renamed the team the St. Patricks. The owners hoped the new name would convince Toronto's large Irish population to attend games.

The St. Patricks reached the Stanley Cup Final in 1922. Standing in their way once again were the Millionaires. And just like in 1918, the series went to five games. Toronto beat Vancouver and won the Cup. Right winger Babe Dye scored nine goals in the series for Toronto.

Conn Smythe bought the Maple Leafs in 1927 and gave the team its current name.

In 1927, Conn Smythe bought the team. Big changes followed. Previously, the team's colors had been green and white. Smythe made them blue and white. The team also became known as the Maple Leafs.

Smythe wanted to create a winning culture in Toronto. He did that by making a big trade. In 1930, the Leafs added King Clancy. The star defenseman had won two Stanley Cups with the Ottawa Senators. Smythe thought Clancy could be a spark for the Maple Leafs to make a Cup run of their own.

The deal proved to be worth it. In 1932, Clancy helped the team win its first Cup as the Maple Leafs. Toronto swept the New York Rangers in three games,

## NATIONAL PRIDE

Conn Smythe changed the name of the team to honor the Canadian army. A maple leaf badge was featured on their uniforms during World War I (1914–18). Smythe, a veteran of the war, hoped his team would wear the jersey with pride, honor, and courage.

The Maple Leafs compete against the Boston Bruins in the 1939 Stanley Cup Final.

scoring six goals in each game. The Leafs reached the Final several more times during the 1930s. However, they fell short each time.

**3**

Syl Apps
celebrates
after
winning
the 1942
Stanley
Cup.

# GLORY DAYS

*T*he Maple Leafs returned to the Stanley Cup Final in 1942. However, the Detroit Red Wings won the first three games. And in Game 4, the Leafs were down 3–2. But in the third period, Toronto captain Syl Apps scored the tying goal. A few minutes later, he assisted on the game-winning goal to keep Toronto alive. The Leafs went on to win the series in seven games. That made them the first team to come back from a 3–0 deficit to win a series. It also started the most successful era in team history.

A dynasty appeared to be in the works. However, World War II (1939–1945) was raging in Europe and Asia. Several Leafs players served in the war. Apps was one of them. In his absence, 19-year-old Ted "Teeder" Kennedy stepped up. Kennedy scored a league-high seven goals in the 1945 playoffs. The Leafs defeated the Red Wings in seven games to win another Stanley Cup.

Apps returned for the 1945–46 season. But Kennedy missed much of

Ted Kennedy scored 230 goals during his 14-year career with the Maple Leafs.

the season due to an injury. The two stars finally played together the following season, and the wins piled up. In fact, the duo led Toronto to another championship.

This time, the Leafs defeated their bitter rival, the Montreal Canadiens.

More success and more changes were on the way. In his final season, Apps led Toronto to a sweep over the Red Wings to win the Stanley Cup in 1948.

Kennedy took over as captain the next season. The Leafs defeated the Red Wings once again. That made Toronto the first team in the NHL era to win three straight Stanley Cups.

## THE BARILKO CURSE

Bill Barilko scored the game-winning goal in the 1951 Stanley Cup Final. Four months later, he went missing after a plane crash. His disappearance led to a myth. Fans said the Leafs couldn't win another Cup until Barilko's body was found. Toronto finally won another championship in 1962. Six weeks later, Barilko's remains were found.

The Leafs celebrate after winning the 1962 Stanley Cup.

Superstar Dave Keon arrived in 1960. He led the Leafs to another three-peat. Toronto won the Stanley Cup in 1962, 1963, and 1964. Fans remember Keon most for his heroics in Game 7 of the 1964 semifinals. He scored a hat trick in a 3–1 victory over the Canadiens.

# DAVE KEON

When Dave Keon arrived in Toronto, winning quickly followed. The star center led the Maple Leafs to a Stanley Cup victory in 1962. That was only Keon's second season in the league. The Leafs ended up winning four Cups in Keon's first seven seasons. After their 1967 win, Keon was awarded the Conn Smythe Trophy. This award is given to the best player in the playoffs.

Keon was small in stature. However, he dominated using his speed and energy. Other players praised him more for what he did without the puck than what he did with it. NHL legend Gordie Howe was impressed with Keon's all-around skill. Former teammate Ron Ellis said he never saw Keon play a bad game.

Keon spent 15 seasons with Toronto. In 2016, the Maple Leafs ranked Keon the best player in team history.

Dave Keon attempts a shot against Detroit Red Wings goalie Terry Sawchuk.

**4**

Leafs defenseman Jim McKenny battles for control of the puck during a 1976 playoff game.

# WRONG SIDE OF HISTORY

The Maple Leafs made regular playoff appearances in the 1970s. Led by Darryl Sittler, the team got all the way to the semifinals in 1978. Unfortunately for Toronto fans, the Leafs lost to the Canadiens.

After years of playoff failures, the Leafs knew they needed a change. Cliff Fletcher took over as the team's general manager in 1991. Fletcher made a 10-player trade with the Calgary Flames. The deal brought center Doug Gilmour to the Maple Leafs. Gilmour went on to lead the team with 127 points in the 1992–93 season.

The Leafs faced the Los Angeles Kings in the 1993 conference final. That series still haunts Toronto fans. In Game 6, Kings superstar Wayne Gretzky hit Gilmour with a high stick in overtime. However, no penalty was called. Gretzky then went on to score the winning goal. The series ended up going to Game 7. Gretzky had three goals and an assist to help clinch a win for the Kings.

The Leafs returned to the semifinals three more times in the next nine years.

Wendel Clark scores a goal during Game 6 of the 1993 conference final.

But each time, they fell short. Every year, Toronto's 1967 championship felt further away.

Starting in 2006, the Leafs missed the playoffs for seven straight years. It marked the worst stretch in team history. The low point came in 2015–16, when Toronto finished in last place. But that awful season came with a reward. The Leafs ended up with the first pick in the 2016 draft. They used it on center Auston Matthews. Along with young stars William Nylander and Mitch Marner, Matthews led the team to immediate success.

In the 2020–21 season, Matthews scored 41 goals. That led the NHL. The Leafs met the Canadiens in the first round of the playoffs. After Toronto took a 3–1 lead in the series, disaster struck again.

## •END OF AN ERA

The Leafs began playing at Maple Leaf Gardens in November 1931. It didn't take long for the team to enjoy success there. Just five months later, Toronto won the Stanley Cup at the Gardens. The Leafs' last game at the historic building took place on February 13, 1999. A week later, the team began playing in its new home, Scotiabank Arena.

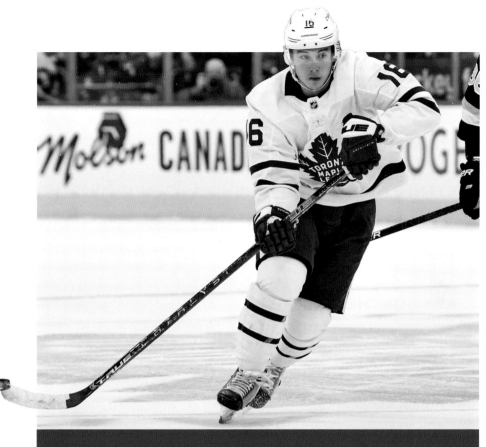

Toronto right winger Mitch Marner skates with the puck during a 2021 game against the Boston Bruins.

The Canadiens won the next three games and eliminated the Leafs. It was another disappointing end for Toronto fans. Even so, the core of talented young players gave them hope for the future.

# • TORONTO MAPLE LEAFS
# QUICK STATS

**FOUNDED:** 1917

**STANLEY CUP CHAMPIONSHIPS:** 13 (1918, 1922, 1932, 1942, 1945, 1947, 1948, 1949, 1951, 1962, 1963, 1964, 1967)

**KEY COACHES:**

• Dick Irvin (1931–40): 216 wins, 152 losses, 59 ties

• Hap Day (1940–50): 259 wins, 206 losses, 81 ties

• Punch Imlach (1958–69, 1981): 370 wins, 275 losses, 125 ties

**HOME ARENA:** Scotiabank Arena (Toronto, ON)

**MOST CAREER POINTS:** Mats Sundin (987)

**MOST CAREER GOALS:** Mats Sundin (420)

**MOST CAREER ASSISTS:** Börje Salming (620)

**MOST CAREER SHUTOUTS:** Turk Broda (61)

*Stats are accurate through the 2020–21 season.*

# GLOSSARY

**ASSIST**
A pass that results in a goal.

**CAPTAIN**
A team's leader.

**DEBUT**
First appearance.

**DRAFT**
An event that allows teams to choose new players coming into the league.

**DYNASTY**
A team that has an extended period of success, usually winning multiple championships in the process.

**HAT TRICK**
A game in which a player scores three or more goals.

**MYTH**
A well-known story that may not be entirely true.

**PENALTY**
A punishment for breaking the rules of the game.

**RIVAL**
An opposing player or team that brings out the greatest emotion from fans and players.

# ● TO LEARN
# *MORE*

## BOOKS

Duling, Kaitlyn. *Women in Hockey*. Lake Elmo, MN: Focus Readers, 2020.

Frederick, Shane. *Auston Matthews: Hockey Dynamo*. North Mankato, MN: Capstone Press, 2020.

Hewson, Anthony K. *GOATs of Hockey*. Minneapolis: Abdo Publishing, 2022.

## MORE INFORMATION

To learn more about the Toronto Maple Leafs, go to **pressboxbooks.com/AllAccess.**

These links are routinely monitored and updated to provide the most current information available.

## INDEX